Have Fun with Arts and Crafts

Tractors and Trucks

Rita Storey

A⁺

Smart Apple Media

Published by Smart Apple Media,
an imprint of Black Rabbit Books
P.O. Box 3263, Mankato, Minnesota 56002
www.blackrabbitbooks.com

Published by arrangement with the
Watts Publishing Group LTD, London.

Library of Congress Cataloging-in-Publication Data

Storey, Rita.
Tractors and trucks / by Rita Storey.
p. cm.—(Have fun with arts and crafts)
Audience: K to grade 3.

Summary: "Provides step by step instructions to create tractor and truck-themed crafts from everyday household
objects. Easy-to-follow directions for a milk tanker, car transporter, and much more are included. Also features a
recipe for a trucker's lunch and instructions to make and play a board game"—Provided by publisher.

Includes index.
ISBN 978-1-59920-901-2 (library binding)
1. Handicraft—Juvenile literature. 2. Tractors—Juvenile literature.
3. Trucks—Juvenile literature. I. Title.
TT160.S76 2014
745.5--dc23
2012042906

Packaged for Franklin Watts by Storeybooks
rita@storeybooks.co.uk
Designer: Rita Storey
Editor: Nicola Barber
Crafts: Rita Storey
Photography: Tudor Photography, Banbury
www.tudorphotography.co.uk

Cover images Wishlistimages (top left), Tudor Photography, Banbury

Before You Start

Some of the projects in this book require scissors, paint, glue, a sewing
needle, and an oven. When using these things, we recommend
that children are supervised by a responsible adult.

Printed in the United States at Corporate Graphics, North Mankato, Minnesota
PO1588
2-2013

9 8 7 6 5 4 3 2 1

Contents

Big Blue Tractor

E very farmer needs a strong tractor to do the hard work on the farm. A tractor is great for digging, pulling, lifting, and pushing heavy loads. Make this bright blue tractor to drive around your farm.

To make a big blue tractor, you will need

- 2 small rectangular cardboard boxes, 1 smaller than the other
- masking tape
- large sheet of paper
- felt-tip pen
- ruler
- scissors
- glue
- crayons
- black and blue paints and paintbrush
- 2 pairs of black lids—1 pair larger than the other (you could use lids from peanut butter containers and jelly jars)
- colored paper

1 Tape all the covers of the cardboard boxes closed. If the boxes are shiny, cover them with masking tape so the paint will stick.

2 Place the larger of the two cardboard boxes on the paper with the biggest side facing up. Use the ruler and felt-tip pen to draw around the box. Do the same with the smaller box, and cut out the shapes. Set these pieces of paper aside.

3 Paint the boxes blue and allow them to dry.

4 Spread glue on the long side of the small box. Glue the small box to the long, thin side of the larger box near the bottom.

5 While the paint is drying, trim the pieces of paper (cut in step 2) so that they are narrower at the top. Using the crayons, draw a black line around the edge of each piece to look like tractor cab windows. Add controls like the ones above.

6 Glue the pieces of paper onto either side of the larger box.

7 Cut four circles out of colored paper. Glue one circle on to the center of each lid.

9 Cut out a ladder and radiator grille shape from the paper left over in step 2. Paint the shapes black and allow them to dry. Glue the grille shape on the front of the tractor. Glue the ladder on to one side of the tractor.

8 Spread glue on the lids, and stick them to the boxes to make wheels.

Chug, chug, chug, chug, chug, chug.

Terrific Tractors

Modern tractors are used to spray crops, sow seeds, and pull mowers. They can also move snow or piles of dirt. Some tractors have huge wheels while others have caterpillar tracks around the wheels. Tractors are very good for driving across muddy or wet ground without getting stuck.

Dig It!

Tractors can have a variety of attachments for different jobs. This tractor has attachments that move just like the real thing. It has a bucket to scoop up dirt or carry building materials, and it has a loader to push rocks and soil into a pile.

To make this tractor, you will need

- felt-tip pen
- 8 in. x 8 in. (20 cm x 20 cm) thin yellow cardstock
- scissors
- glue
- 8 in. x 8 in. (20 cm x 20 cm) thin black cardstock
- 8 in. x 8 in. (20 cm x 20 cm) thin red cardstock
- glue
- 8 paper fasteners

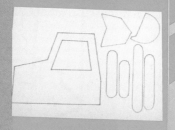

1 Using the felt-tip pen, draw the shapes of the tractor arms, bucket, and loader on the yellow cardstock. See page 30 for the templates.

2 Cut out the shapes.

3 Using the templates on page 30, cut out two tractor wheels from the black cardstock, one larger than the other. Cut two circles of red cardstock that are smaller than the black circles.

4 Glue the red circles on to the middle of the black circles to make wheels.

5 Push a paper fastener through the center of the larger of the wheels and then through the cab of the tractor just below the window. Open the paper fastener.

6 Push a paper fastener through the center of the smaller wheel and then through the front of the tractor level with the back wheel. Open the paper fastener.

7 Join the two pieces of the back arm together with a paper fastener.

8 Attach the bucket shape to the arm with a paper fastener.

9 Repeat steps 7 and 8 with the front arm and loader attachment.

10 Using a paper fastener, attach the front arm to the front of the tractor.

11 Using a paper fastener, attach the back arm to the back of the tractor.

Dig, dig, dig with this great yellow tractor!

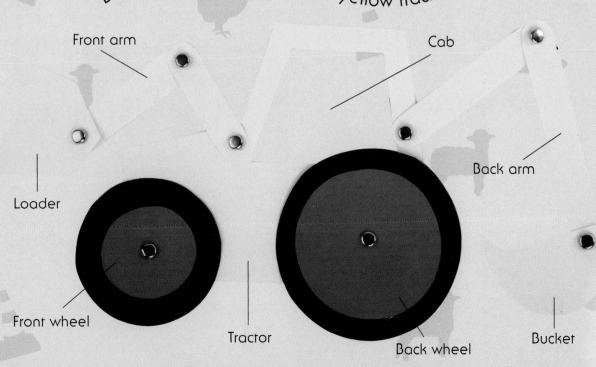

Front arm

Cab

Back arm

Loader

Front wheel

Tractor

Back wheel

Bucket

Working in the Fields

You can often see tractors pulling plows in the countryside. Imagine a country scene with little fields of different colors and textures. Decorate your fields with different patterns, and put your toy tractors to work.

To make a textured field picture, you will need

- 11 in. x 17 in. (29 cm x 43 cm) sheet of thick paper cut into 12 squares, 4 in. x 4 in. (10 cm x 10 cm)
  - paints and paintbrushes
    - glue
  - seeds, sand, leaves
- green and yellow tissue paper
  - cotton balls
  - felt-tip pen
  - mesh canvas
- sheet of thick paper larger than 17 in. x 17 in. (43 cm x 43 cm)

1 Paint the squares of thick paper in shades of green and brown. Allow them to dry. Decorate each piece with a different field pattern.

2 Spread glue on a green background in lines or all over. Scatter seeds on the glue and tap any remaining seeds off.

3 Ball up small pieces of green tissue paper. Glue them in lines on a brown background to look like crops or along the edges of the fields to make hedges.

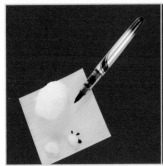

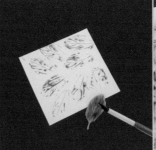

4 Roll pieces of cotton balls into small balls and glue them on to a green square. Using a felt-tip pen, draw legs and a face to look like sheep.

5 Paint three wavy lines or three diagonal lines of glue on a brown background. Scatter sand on the glue. Tap off any sand that does not stick.

6 Paint the back of a leaf and press it on to a yellow background.

7 Small pieces of yellow tissue paper crumpled into balls make good sunflowers.

8 Glue strips of mesh canvas around a green square to look like fences around a meadow.

9 Glue all the squares onto a large sheet of thick paper.

Can you think of anything else to use to make crop textures?

Watch your toy tractors hard at work in the fields.

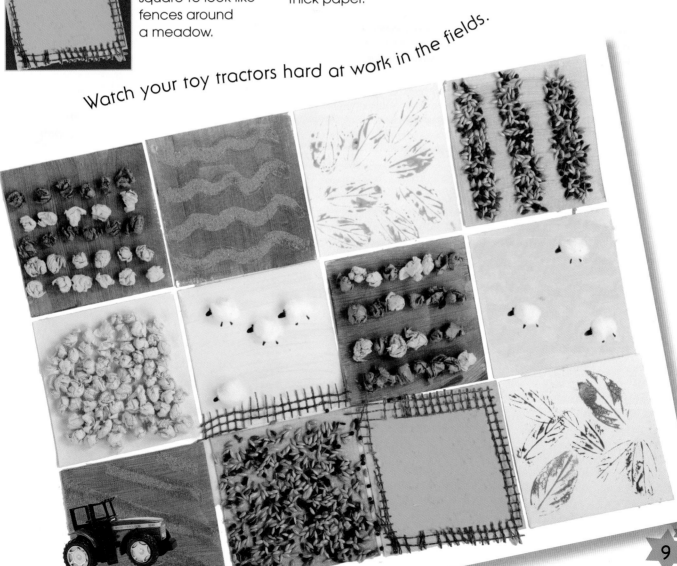

Tractor Tire Tracks

Tractors have thick tires that can grip in mud or on snow and ice. The tires have different patterns on their treads. You can make your own tire tread designs to print a great tractor tire pattern image.

To make a tractor tire image, you will need

- felt-tip pen
- scissors
- foam sheet
- 8.5 in. x 11 in. (21 cm x 29 cm) sheets of thick paper (white or colored)
- cardboard tube from the inside of a roll of paper towels
- glue
- paintbrush
- clear tape
- baking tray
- scrap of cardboard
- paint
- scrap paper
- large sheet of white paper

1 Using the templates on page 31, copy the shapes and draw them on to the foam sheet with a felt-tip pen. Cut out the shapes.

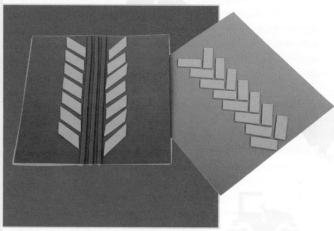

2 Cut a piece of thick paper narrower than the length of the cardboard tube and wide enough to wrap around it. Brush some glue on the back of each shape and glue them on to the paper in a pattern like the ones in the picture above. Allow it to dry.

3 With the shapes on the outside, roll the paper around the tube and secure with clear tape.

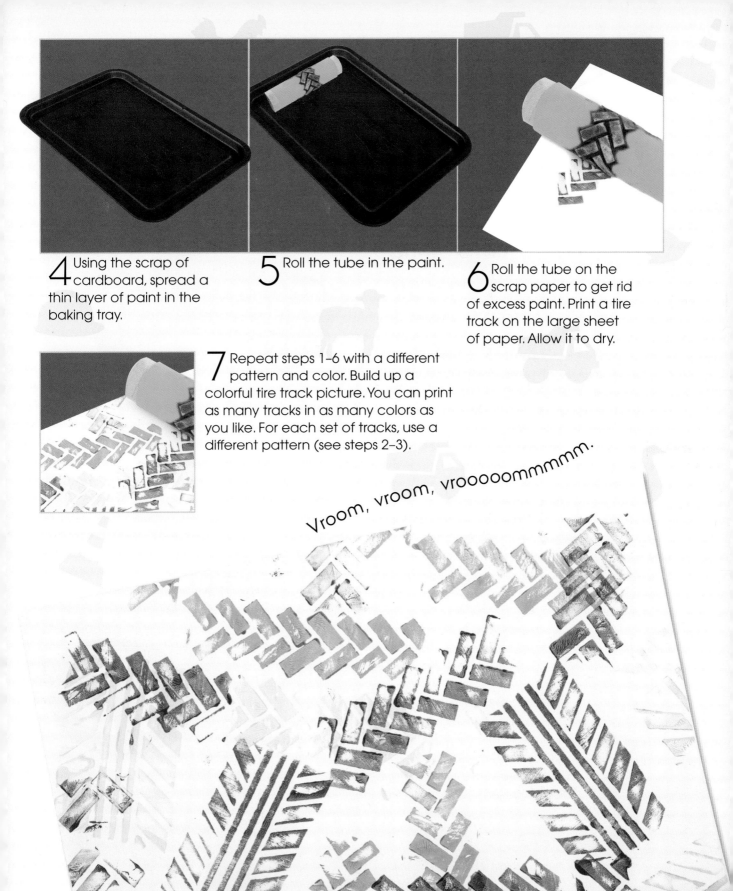

4 Using the scrap of cardboard, spread a thin layer of paint in the baking tray.

5 Roll the tube in the paint.

6 Roll the tube on the scrap paper to get rid of excess paint. Print a tire track on the large sheet of paper. Allow it to dry.

7 Repeat steps 1–6 with a different pattern and color. Build up a colorful tire track picture. You can print as many tracks in as many colors as you like. For each set of tracks, use a different pattern (see steps 2–3).

Vroom, vroom, vroooooommmmm.

Truck Cab

To make the dashboard of a big rig, grab a large cardboard box and some paint. Use your imagination to find odds and ends that can be used to make levers, buttons, joysticks, and switches. Drive your big rig anywhere you like!

To make a dashboard, you will need

- large cardboard box
- scissors
- paint and paintbrush
- clear tape
- black poster board
- compass and pencil
- ruler
- cardboard tube
- glue
- small butter lid
- a selection of lids and tops from bottles or jelly jars
- colored paper
- telephone cord
- empty matchbox

1 Flatten out the cardboard box and cut off the top. Cut off one side. Paint the inside of the box.

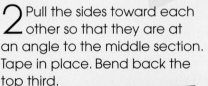

2 Pull the sides toward each other so that they are at an angle to the middle section. Tape in place. Bend back the top third.

3 Set the compass to 4.75 in. (12 cm) and draw a circle on the black poster board. Keep the point in the same place, but change the compass to 3 in. (8 cm). Draw a circle inside the first. Keep the point in the same place, but change the compass to 1.5 in. (3.8 cm). Draw another circle inside the first two. Cut around the largest circle line.

4 Lay the ruler with the end on the small circle. Draw a line on either side of it. Repeat twice more evenly spacing around the wheel. The lines you draw should make the shape of a big *Y*. Cut out between the lines as shown here.

5 Cut one end off the cardboard tube at an angle. Cut slits ½ in. (1 cm) long and ¼ in. (5 mm) apart all the way around both ends. Bend back the tabs.

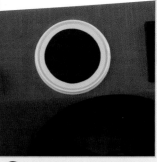

6 Paint the tube black. Glue the tabs on the straight end of the tube to the back of the steering wheel.

7 Spread glue on the tabs of the angled end of the tube.

8 Position the steering wheel on the base of the box so the wheel is angled toward you. Glue a circle of colored paper to a jelly jar lid to make a horn. Glue it to the center of the wheel.

9 Use the compass to draw a circle on the black paper the size of the inner circle of the butter container. Cut out the circle and glue it on to the lid. Brush glue on the back of the lid and glue it on the dashboard to make a speedometer.

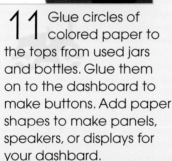

10 If you can find an old piece of telephone cord, attach an empty matchbox to the end with tape. Paint the matchbox black, and you have a CB radio handset.

11 Glue circles of colored paper to the tops from used jars and bottles. Glue them on to the dashboard to make buttons. Add paper shapes to make panels, speakers, or displays for your dashbard.

That's a Big 10–4!

Truckers use Citizen Band radio (CB for short) to talk to each other from their cabs. Rather than using their real names, CB radio users have "handles" (nicknames). They also have unusual words and expressions for CB radio—read some of them in the CB Radio Glossary on page 32.

Magnetic Tractor Game

Tractors work hard pulling plows and carrying heavy loads around farms. How quickly can your tractor get a bale of hay to the sheep in the farthest field?

To make a magnetic tractor game, you will need

- pair of magnets
- tape
- ruler
- toy tractor
- 12 in. x 17 in. (30 cm x 43 cm) piece of cardboard
- paint or felt-tip pens
- 4 bottle tops (all the same size)
- glue
- watch or stopwatch
- small candies or toy hay bale

To make each sheep
- square of thin cardstock 3 in. x 3 in. (8 cm x 8 cm)
- glue
- cotton balls
- googly eyes

Board

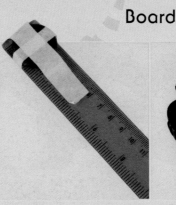

1 Tape one half of the magnet to the end of the ruler.

2 Tape the other half of the magnet underneath the tractor.

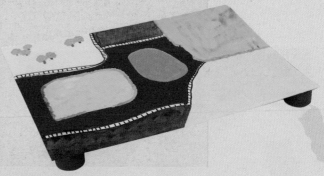

3 Draw or paint a farm track a bit wider than the tractor on to the cardboard. Include some tight turns. Paint the farm around the track. Glue the four bottle tops to the underside of the track, one in each corner.

Sheep

4 Fold the square of card in half. Draw your sheep on the card, making sure ¾ in. (2 cm) of the back of the sheep is along the fold at the top. Cut out your sheep, but don't cut along the fold.

5 Pull the cotton ball in half. Glue half of the cotton ball on each side of the body of the sheep. Glue on a googly eye. Make as many sheep as you need.

14

To Play the Game

1 Slide the end of the ruler with the magnet attached under the track. Put the tractor on the start of the track above it. Move the ruler along under the track and watch the tractor move above it.

2 Load the tractor bucket with some food for the sheep (a toy hay bale or a piece of candy). Follow track to the field of sheep. Drop off the load.

3 Can you make it to the field without dropping the load? Try timing yourself with the second hand of a watch or a stopwatch.

Tape the magnet on a truck and draw roads instead of a farm scene to play a truck challenge game too.

Ask your friends to take the challenge. You could try making more circuits and adding some extra cargo on each one. If you are playing the game using candy, the winner can eat the candy!

Notebook Truck Graphics

Trucks are often covered in colorful and sometimes crazy graphics. Create your own zany graphic sign and turn a plain notebook into a really funky one.

To make notebook truck graphics, you will need

- sheet of white paper
- sheet of colored paper the same size as your notebook
- felt-tip pens
- scissors
- crayons
- newspapers and magazines
- glue
- stick-on stars
- notebook
- clear adhesive film

1 On a sheet of paper, draw some flames the width of the paper. See page 30 for a template to copy. Using crayons, color in the flames.

2 Many truck graphics include an animal. Cut out a picture from a magazine or draw one on colored paper. Cut out a circle around the animal. Cut out a truck from a magazine or draw one of your own.

3 Glue the flames onto the sheet of colored paper. Glue the circle containing the animal near the top of the flames. Glue the truck at the bottom. Allow it to dry.

4 Cut around the edge of the shape. Follow the shape, but leave a border all the way around.

Truck Wraps

The amazing graphics on trucks and trailers are often designed on a computer and printed out onto sheets of thin, sticky-backed vinyl. The printed sheets are carefully stuck onto each panel of the truck or trailer.

5 Glue the shape to the front of a notebook. Finish your picture by adding on some stars. Cover the picture with clear adhesive film.

Milk Tanker

Milk tankers collect fresh milk from farms every day. They take it to a plant where it is treated. Some of it is put into cartons, ready to go to the supermarket. You can make this milk tanker ready for the next milk collection.

To make a milk tanker, you will need

- large cardboard tube
- sheet of white paper as wide as the tube and long enough to wrap around it
- clear tape
- sheet of colored paper as wide as the tube and long enough to wrap half way around it
- scissors
- pencil
- black paint
- red paint
- glue
- 2 rubber bands
- 5 small cardboard tubes
- black paper
- small cardboard box
- paintbrush
- silver paper
- white paper
- felt-tip pen

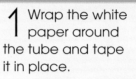

1 Wrap the white paper around the tube and tape it in place.

2 Using the template on page 31, cut both the long edges of the colored paper into a curved shape.

3 Glue the colored paper on to the tube. Hold in place with two rubber bands. When the glue is dry, remove the rubber bands.

4 Draw around the end of the small cardboard tube on to the black paper. Repeat 10 times. Cut out each circle 1/8 in. (3 mm) wider than the circles you have drawn.

5 Paint the tubes black. Allow them to dry.

6 Paint glue on the top edge of one of the tubes.

7 Press the glued edge on to a circle of paper. Do the same on the other end. Repeat with the rest of the tubes.

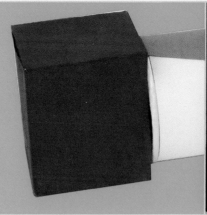

8 Paint the small box red. Allow it to dry.

9 Glue one end of the large tube to the box.

10 Glue the small tubes to the bottom of your tanker. Glue one tube under the cab and two pairs under the large tube.

11 Cut 10 circles of silver paper. Glue one in the middle of each wheel. Allow everything to dry.

12 Cut out the shape of a windshield and a front grille from white paper (like the ones on the milk tanker below). Draw horizontal lines on the front grille with a felt-tip pen.

Hit the road with this awesome milk tanker!

Car Transporter

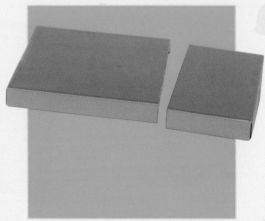

Car transporters deliver new cars across the country. The back of this model car transporter folds down so that you can drive your toy cars up the ramp. Fill it up and make an express delivery.

To make this car transporter, you will need

- shoe box with lid
- scissors
- duct tape
- paint
- paintbrush
- colored paper
- black and red cardstock
- glue

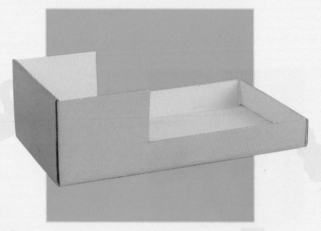

1 Cut across the lid of the shoe box, one-third of the way along.

2 Cut a section out of the shoe box. It needs to be the same length as the long piece of the lid. Cut two-thirds of the way down the box and then along to the end.

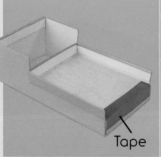

Tape

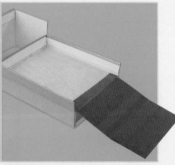

3 Turn the larger section of the lid around and attach the cut end to the back of the transporter with duct tape.

4 Trim one of the pieces of cardboard that was cut from the side of the box to be the same width as the lid. Tape it on to the back of the truck to make a ramp.

5 Tape the smaller section of the lid to the front of the box to form the cab.

6 Paint the transporter. Allow it to dry. Cut strips of colored paper and glue them on to decorate the transporter.

7 Cut out circles of black cardstock and glue them on to the bottom of the car transporter to make wheels. Cut out circles of red cardstock and glue them on to the middle of the wheels.

Drive your toy cars up the ramp and make some deliveries.

Trucker's Lunch

Truckers need a good packed lunch to keep them going on those long journeys. Make yourself a tasty trucker's lunch.

To make a trucker's lunch, you will need

Truck Rolls

• 2 white bread rolls • butter • knife
• 2 slices of cheese or ham
• 6 cherry tomatoes
• 6 slices of cucumber
• 6 toothpicks (with the sharp ends removed)

Traffic Light Fruit Kebabs

• 3 red fruits: grapes, strawberries, or cherries (pits removed)
• 3 orange fruits: orange segments or cubes of melon
• 3 green fruits: grapes or slices of kiwi
• 3 toothpicks (with the sharp ends removed)
• kitchen knife

Rocky Road

• ¼ cup (125 g) butter
• 10.5 oz. (300 g) milk chocolate, broken into pieces
• 3 Tbsp (45 mL) corn syrup
• 14 graham crackers
• 2 cups (100 g) mini marshmallows
• powdered sugar
• bowl • saucepan • wooden spoon
• plastic bag • rolling pin
• baking pan, 9 in. x 13 in. (23 cm x 33 cm)
• spatula • kitchen knife

A Truck Roll

1 Slice both of the rolls in half lengthways and spread both halves with butter. Place the ham or cheese slices on one half of the roll. Put the top half of the roll on top of the filling.

2 Cut the rolls two-thirds of the way along. Cut the cucumber slices in half. Cut the tomatoes in half through the middle.

Take out the toothpicks when you eat the rolls.

3 Thread a half cucumber slice and half a tomato on to a toothpick and push the toothpick through the rolls. Push a slice of cucumber and a tomato on the other side. Repeat with all the tomatoes and cucumber to make three sets of wheels for your truck roll.

Traffic Light Fruit Kebabs

1 To make a red–orange–green traffic light, thread a red fruit, an orange fruit, and a green fruit onto a toothpick.

Rocky Road

1 Put the butter, chocolate pieces, and corn syrup in to a bowl. Put some water into the saucepan. Rest the bowl on the saucepan. The bowl must not touch the water. Put the pan on a low heat. Stir with a wooden spoon until everything is melted. Take the pan off the heat.

2 Put the graham crackers into a plastic bag and tap the bag gently with the rolling pin until there are some crumbs and a few larger chunks.

3 Pour the melted chocolate mixture into a bowl. Add the graham cracker pieces and crumbs to the melted mixture. Add the marshmallows. Stir everything together.

4 Pour the mixture into a baking pan and smooth the top with the wooden spoon. Put the pan in the refrigerator for 2 to 3 hours. When the mixture has set, sprinkle with powdered sugar and cut into squares.

Ask an adult to help you with step 1 of the Rocky Road recipe.

Monster Truck Driver

If you want to drive a truck of your own, now is your chance. Find a picture of yourself and put it in the driving seat of this cool monster truck card.

To make this truck card, you will need

- 8.5 in. x 11 in. (21 cm x 29 cm) sheet of stiff paper
- scissors
- masking tape
- cardstock
- thick paints and stiff paintbrushes
- felt-tip pens
- glitter glue
- small photograph of yourself to put in the driver's seat

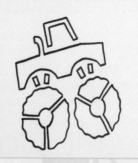

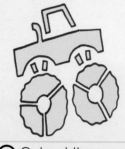

1 Trace the shape on page 31 on to a sheet of stiff paper.

2 Cut out the sections shown in blue to create a truck stencil. (This is a bit fussy, so ask an adult to help).

3 Using masking tape, tape the stencil to a sheet of cardstock so that the stencil covers the bottom half of the card.

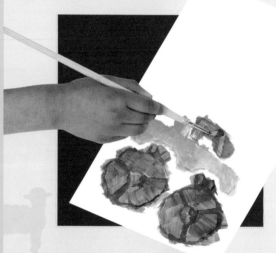

4 Use thick paint and a stiff brush to paint through the stencil onto the card.

5 Carefully peel off the stencil. When it is dry, you can use the stencil again to make another card.

6 Fold the card in half so the truck is on the front.

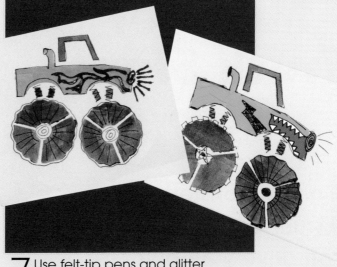

7 Use felt-tip pens and glitter glue to decorate your truck.

8 Cut out your photo to fit in the cab window. Glue it in to the window.

Make a card for a friend, so they can be a monster truck driver too!

Monster Truck Stunt Game

In this monster truck stunt game, you can drive your own monster truck around a crazy track. Challenge a friend to play and "put the pedal to the metal" in a race for the finish line—doing some amazing freestyle stunts on the way.

To make and play the monster truck stunt game, you will need

- colored paper
- coin
- felt-tip pen
- scissors
- 11 in. x 17 in. (28 cm x 43 cm) sheet of cardstock
- glue
- thick white paper
- crayons
- die

1 Draw around the coin on to the colored paper 20 times.

2 Cut out the circles.

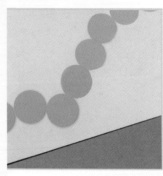

3 Glue the colored circles on to the cardstock. The circles need to touch but you can make a wiggly line going across the card.

4 Draw flashes like the ones shown. Color them with crayons. Cut them out and glue them on to as many circles as you want. Make sure you glue one on each end of the line.

5 Number the circles 1–20 as shown, from the top left. Decorate the board with cutout monster truck pictures. Write "Winner" on circle 20.

6 Write instructions on the circles and flashes. Think up some of your own, or use these:

- Jump 3 cars (move forward 3 spaces)
- Squash 2 cars (miss a turn)
- Crazy crash, but keep going (miss a turn)
- Wipe out. Game over!
- Flip the truck (move to the next circle)

7 To make the counters: draw around the coin onto the thick white paper until you have one circle for each player. Cut the circles out. Draw a monster truck on each counter, each one a different color, or cut out trucks from a magazine and glue them on.

Use these instructions, but you can find or draw pictures of semis for another fun truck game!

Monster Trucks

Monster trucks are customized trucks with huge wheels and crazy graphics. They race, jump, crush cars, perform freestyle displays, and do other crazy stunts.

How to Play the Game

Each player has a counter and puts it on the first circle. The first player rolls the die. Move the counter the number of circles shown on the die. If there is an instruction on the circle, do as it says. Take turns rolling the die. The winner is the first one to reach the finish line by rolling the exact number to land on circle 20.

27

Mosaic Pictures

Build mosaic pictures of a fire engine and a colorful tractor. These will look great on your bedroom wall.

To make mosaic pictures, you will need

Fire Engine

- sheets of red, black, yellow, and orange paper
- scissors
- yellow background paper
- glue

Tractor

- sheets of yellow, black, red, brown, and cream paper
- scissors
- purple background paper
- glue

Fire Engine

1 Cut the red paper into strips ½ in. (1 cm) wide.

2 Cut the strips into lots of squares ½ in. x ½ in. (1 cm x 1 cm).

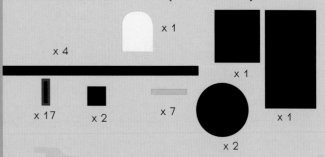

x 4   x 1   x 1

x 17   x 2   x 7   x 1

x 2

3 Copy the shapes above and cut them out to make the ladders, wheels, doors, windows, and bumpers.

4 Place the squares on a piece of paper to make a picture of a fire engine. Add a dab of glue to the back of each piece and glue in position.

Keep the paper on a flat surface and away from any drafts until you have glued all the squares in place.

Tractor

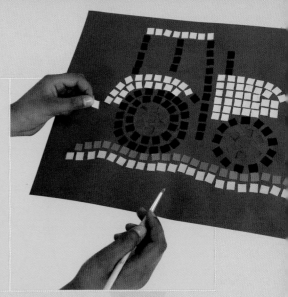

1 Cut the colored paper into strips ½ in. (1 cm) wide.

2 Cut the strips into lots of squares ½ in. x ½ in. (1 cm x 1 cm).

3 Place the squares on a piece of paper to build up a picture of a tractor. Add a dab of glue to the back of each piece and glue in position.

Cut more squares and make your name part of your mosaic.

29

Templates

Dig It!
Pages 6–7

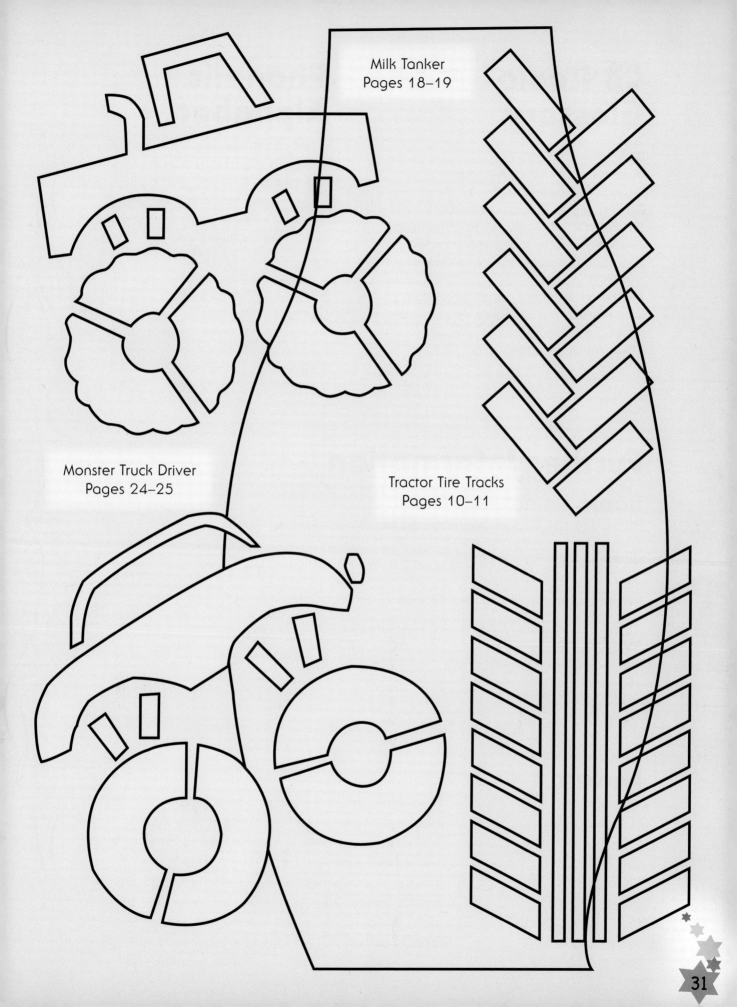

Milk Tanker
Pages 18–19

Monster Truck Driver
Pages 24–25

Tractor Tire Tracks
Pages 10–11

CB Radio Glossary

Bear police officer
Bear in the air police helicopter
Big rig 18-wheel truck
Do you copy? Do you understand?
Breaker 19 what you say to other users
   when you want to use the channel
Over and out done talking and turning off
   the CB
Put the pedal to the metal accelerate
Your handle the nickname you use when
   using a CB radio
10-4 message understood

Phonetic Alphabet

Not all truckers use this alphabet, but it helps to spell things out on crackly radio reception. Can you spell out your name using the alphabet below?

Lucy = Lima – Uniform – Charlie – Yankee
Sam = Sierra – Alpha – Mike

A = Alpha	J = Juliet	S = Sierra
B = Bravo	K = Kilo	T = Tango
C = Charlie	L = Lima	U = Uniform
D = Delta	M = Mike	V = Victor
E = Echo	N = November	W = Whiskey
F = Foxtrot	O = Oscar	X = X-ray
G = Golf	P = Papa	Y = Yankee
H = Hotel	Q = Quebec	Z = Zulu
I = India	R = Romeo	

Further Information

Books

Nixon, James. *Tractors (Machines on the Move)*. Amicus, 2011

Nixon, James. *Trucks (Machines on the Move)*. Amicus, 2011

Parrish, Margaret. *Trucks and Diggers (Wild Rides)*. New Forest Press, 2013

Websites

http://www.playtruckgames.org/

Index